T0208482

Wild Asters

Wild Asters

Judith Hishikawa

WILD ASTERS

iUniverse books may be ordered through booksellers or by contacting:

iUniverse
1663 Liberty Drive
Bloomington, IN 47403
www.iuniverse.com
1-800-Authors (1-800-288-4677)

ISBN: 978-1-6632-0053-2 (sc)
ISBN: 978-1-6632-0054-9 (e)

Print information available on the last page.

iUniverse rev. date: 05/12/2020

Contents

Introduction

Upon moving to the city, from a log cabin in the north woods of Vermont the writer thought: "Oh, no, my haiku will suffer!"

She then took this statement as a challenge.

From February 2019

I dance
with
emptiness

from a cloudy sky
it rains
without purpose

love is a fever
a light dream continues
then fades

gone
the unrecoverable past
east river flows

           the rhythm of waves
        the movement of the moon
          reverberate inside

between us
unbreakable
a wall

gentle wind
blowing in and out
a frequent visitor

squirrels
strip the buds
bare stalks

the moon moves
slowly, perceptively
through bare branches

unexpected
shelf fungus
Broadway cherry tree

city snow
remarkably like
Vermont snow

brown pigeon
flying alone
chimney pots

space a premium
kitchen bicycle
foggy sky

              silent walk
            embraced by rain
              I dance

girl on the beach
absorbed in her phone
puppy's stick not tossed

              reeds grow
             in roof top
              puddles

Central Park

aluminum rowboats
keep the pace, keep the pace
oars squeak

                        on the rocks
                    turtles and people
                    sunning themselves

children of nature
all sizes and shapes
first warm day

trees and butterflies
hold the skyscrapers
in check

                        a girl alone
                    rowing backwards
                     long black hair

canopy of green
elm sentinels
shield their statues

cascades of seed capsules
elms shower down
their future

Manhattan's core
revealed in the park
shiny and bold

windy day
skinny skyscraper's
upper floors

impossible perch
high crane lifts
a dark bundle

after a tunnel
trees and blue sky
fresh air

saxophone
musicians lift the breeze
heralding spring

dreamers
too soon for ice cream
yet it is consumed

                              clusters
                    mothers and children
                       pose for a portrait

strand bookstall
tables of old friends
traffic halts

an arsenal
armed no more
metal eagles

                    unexpected
            a butterfly shopping bag
            pops from a change purse

Upper West Side

doorman on duty
gazes wistfully
towards the park

little dogs galore
then two fine collies
upper west side

small restaurant
getting smaller
hostess annoyed with humanity

phone charging oasis
the local
public library

mother city
rocks us to sleep
on her trains

Astoria

unpacking
family treasures prevail
iron fry pan, grandfather's level

                    slice of day moon
                    white streaked sky
                    pontoon planes

city ferry
going slow
through Hell Gate

just two goslings left
in spring there were eight
ebb tide

                    teeth up in the gutter
                    last dash across the street
                    furry squirrel

botanical garden
dry stream bed
sunny day

in the laundromat
one reads Ikkyu, one the news
Which one is enlightened?

folding pajamas
opposite an imam folding gowns
white cap on the shelf

wild asters
between the mailboxes
in Astoria

the pain
of an autumn day
clear cold running water

blown by the wind
each stalk dancing its own dance
a clump of asters

breeze tossed
ten inches tall
elm seedlings

arranging
my life
at the kitchen table

sunny day
light breeze in the willows
pale green hydrangeas

fresh sidewalk
pigeons
don't care

blue surprise
hosta blossoms
Socrates Park

city soles
are white
now

on a flatbed truck
brand-new green tractor
Astoria Boulevard

new apartments abound
not old and scruffy
like me

long black cloud
over east river
was this the rain?

smelt fishers
at the ferry terminal
all in hijabs

a splash
from the ferry
wets a library book

                    dark fish
                circle crab nets
                which is the bait?

to the couple
in the laundromat
I'm glad I'm single

urban rips
I wear my farm pants
neat and trim

friendly chatter
with strangers on a bus
refreshes the spirit

sidewalk treasures
passing strangers' smiles
a dancing child

racing motorcycle
old man on a bike
stops to watch

sad little dog
with a clear surgical collar
did you lose something?

Astoria
even the bottle collector
has style

Brief Bio

I grew up in Vermont, lived in Japan as an English teacher, wife, and mother. Eventually, after retirement from the Fort Lee, NJ public school system in 2010, I moved back to a log cabin in the north woods of Vermont for over 8 years. I moved here in February 2019 to be near family.

Please visit my website www.judithhishikawa.com.

Printed in the United States
By Bookmasters